Success with Small Apple Trees

A Companion to *Espalier Made Easy* Webinar

By Mason Vollmer

*"Even if I knew that tomorrow, the world would go to pieces
I would still plant my apple tree"*

- Unknown

*"Those who plant trees are servants of God and faces they've
not met shall call them blessed"*

- Richard St.Barbe Baker

Prologue

If you've ever wanted to have success with small apple trees, or are interested in trying Espalier apple trees in your backyard, school, or community garden – then this book, and the webinar *Espalier Made Easy*, are the tools for you.

Ever since meeting Alan Chadwick in 1974, I've been including Espalier and small apple trees in every educational garden I've helped create ever since. I've distilled the basics for your success.

After an enthusiastic response to my talks on The Art and Science of Espalier in 2022 and 2023, I've put it all together in this booklet and the companion webinar, so that you too may enjoy the joy, beauty, and productivity of well-tended apple trees. The webinar gives a narrative overview, with lots of images, to get started ASAP. This booklet is a reference to go back over, after viewing the webinar, to delve deeper into some of the details.

I've also included the 'Spindle' method, since it can be thought of as an informal Espalier, yet with quicker results and maximum yields that has benefits that anyone interested in taking on Espalier should also know about.

Grow On!

Mason Vollmer 2023

Chapter 1 Training Simplified

Common question I often hear is: *What does my Espalier need?*

The short answer is *Training*. The main structure, or architecture arises from *Leaders* that have been trained into specific geometric forms and predetermined spacing. Alongside this form, are short *Lateral* branches that carry the flowers and fruit.

The most common mistake I see is gardeners trying to winter prune their way to form. Espalier is all about summer branch training of both Leaders and Laterals. In my experience this is harder to teach since it happens over summer when the trees are in leaf and actively growing.

With winter pruning it's easier to see what's going on and it's easier to photograph and diagram. Yet Winter pruning belongs to an older system of orchard care that did all of the pruning in winter because of labor scheduling and cost.

Espalier is for those who like to putter in their garden on a regular basis and don't mind making little adjustments throughout the growing season. When well trained, there is almost no Winter pruning needed.

Pets have become family members and Plants (Indoors and Out) have become the new Pets

One of the most engaging aspects of Espalier is the deepening relationship between the tree and the gardener. The vertical leaders recharge the vigor, while the laterals transform that energy into flower and fruit.

In Module 1, I show how the simplest form is the Single Cordon: One leader with many short laterals.

In Module 2, I show a variation on the vertical Single Cordon as the Oblique Cordon. This was popular in England as a way to keep a row of these lower in height before more dwarfing rootstocks came into wider use.

Also in Module 2, I show additional techniques used to keep apple trees small by training the Single Cordon to variations including: the U with two leaders, the Trident with three leaders, the Double-U with four leaders. And the Belgian Fence, with it's left and right leaders, either U or Double-U, creating an interlocking diamond pattern.

All of these Classical Espalier forms are variations on multiple Leaders and Laterals. In answer to the question : *What does my Espalier need?* The first to get attention is training the leader since this will establish the basic form.

Hand-in-hand in starting any Espalier form is choosing the best rootstock, deciding what form, mapping that out on paper, and transferring that to a suitable trellis. This is covered in Module 2, using the Belgian Fence as an example.

I also point out in Module 2, that the most common Espalier form that I see *"underperforming"* is the 3-Tiered Horizontal form. I've learned this mistake through experience. I've come to see that it is the result of missing the distinct roles that leaders and laterals play. The 3-Tiered Horizontal Espalier often turns into a kind of shadowy hedge, with lower than ideal quality and quantity fruit, giving Espalier a bad impression and leaving many gardeners confused about what went wrong and how to correct it.

Depending on age, condition, rootstock, and vigor, my solution is to convert the 3-Tiered Horizontal Espalier into a Candelabra with either 5 or 7 upright leaders.

Since starter 3-Tiered Horizontal trees are often sold by nurseries, I'm eager to share this solution because *What to do with my Espalier* is easily answered by identifying what to do with the leaders and laterals. This touches on the importance of light management facilitated by adequate spacing of main branches.

Now as promised in the Webinar, we can take a deeper dive into the science and physiology of leaders and laterals in Pome fruits (Apples and Pears) and why Espalier succeeds with these fruits in particular.

Leaders

This diagram of a 2-year old branch in Winter shows five shoots transitioning from the vertical to the horizontal, with 2-year old fruiting spurs below that.

#1

#2

#3

#4

#5

At the tip of #1 is a bud unique to trees with *Apical Dominance.* Within this bud is the Apical Meristem – a region of powerful growth and renewal.

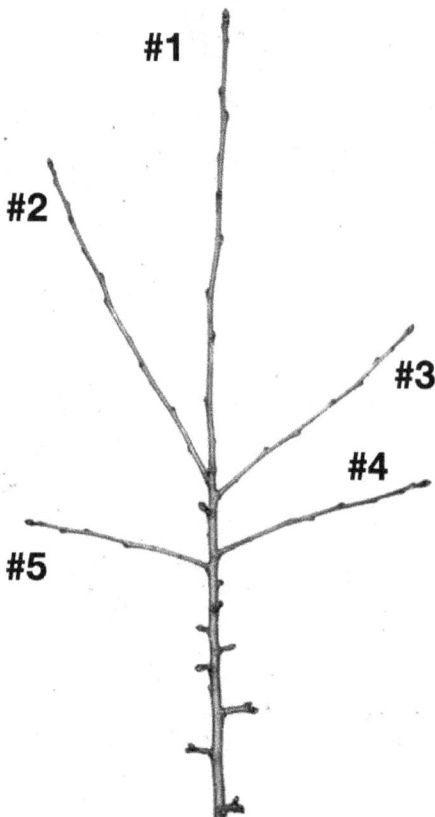

#2 and 3 are *Co-dominant* branches that should be removed entirely as soon as possible. (Reasons are listed in Webinar) And #4 and 5 are terminating not in vegetative buds as in #1, 2, and 3, but floral buds. Yet as shared in Module 1, if you want to split this single leader into two – you can do that by cutting back to #4 and 5. During the summer, raise the weaker #5 to even out growth with #4 and use wire to curve these into the vertical and you'll have a perfect U with two even leaders. To make a Double-U you'll need to spread these further before turning upright and dividing again, in order to maintain ~18" between four upright leaders.

Arborists call this #1-5 pattern shown in the diagram *Branch ordination* among trees with Apical Dominance and is true to most deciduous trees that have evolved in forest settings where competition for light and height is strong. Pruning re-establishes the order and possibly the number and placement of the dominant leader. Make sense?

Throughout the establishment of any Espalier, it is the intentional training and guidance of the leader(s) that the primary scaffold or form is determined. Together with the right selection of rootstock, the tree peaks s at its mature height when the form is complete and is covered in fruit.

A bit of science I left out of the webinar has to do with what Pome fruits are and how they inspired the whole art of espalier.

How Pome fruits are modified wood

You know how tomatoes are fruits and not vegetables? Or how strawberries are not actually berries? It's a botanical thing, based on what plant parts are modified to become attractive to animals. The part we often don't eat in apples, pears, and quince - the core - is to the botanist the true fruit, since it contains the seeds.

In Pome fruits, you have two ends: the stem and the calyx. Just beyond the calyx was the flower. When a fruit forms below the flower, it is called an 'inferior' ovary because of this lower position. To a botanist the core is the actual fruit since it contains the seeds and in Pome fruits it consists of five fused carpels, forming the familiar five pointed star when you cut cross-wise. What we eat, is actually modified wood! The functional seed-bearing fruit has retracted into this sweet modified wood. This is the structure of the *Pome* fruit - apples, pears, and others.

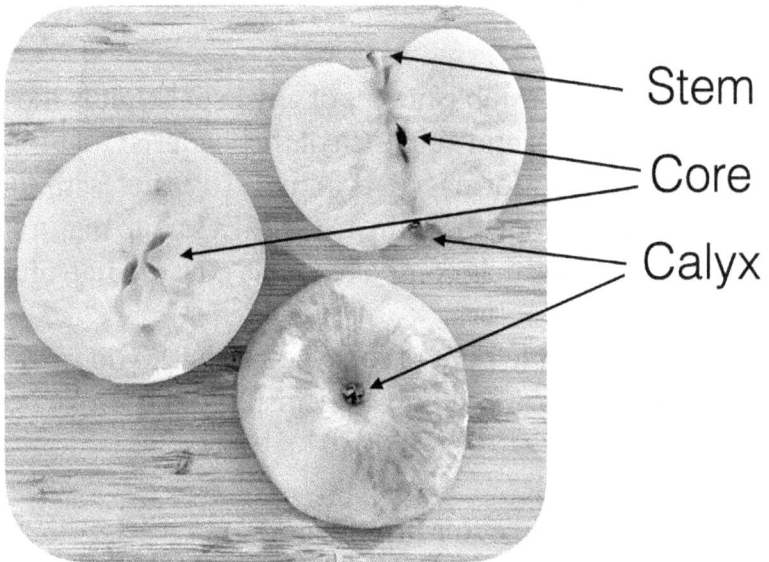

Stem

Core

Calyx

Evolutionary significance of the Pome fruit

This design seems to have given Pome fruits a unique super power, since they are 'woody', the fruits can keep for months under a blanket of autumn leaves and snow. The land of origin for many Pome fruits is in the temperate Northern climate along the Silk Road including modern day Kazakstan and Afghanistan.

This storability endeared them to human beings dealing with ancient Ice Age conditions. By going dormant, deciduous trees are adapted to cold dark winters. Maple trees with their spring sap flow, oaks with their acorns, beech, walnut, and others also became important food sources for early peoples who saw them not merely for their utility but as part of a sacred living nature, who shared abundant life for all.

Ancient gardeners learned how bending down branches accelerated early fruiting and prehistoric gardens contained early forms of Espalier that was later refined by the Romans who brought back choice varieties from the East, which were later cultivated by Monks in the Middle Ages in walled gardens. Even the art of grafting has its origins in an ancient prehistoric era.

With Pome fruits, the more they fruit, the less they shoot - and this leads to smaller, more manageable trees. The fact that the laterals can be maintained as short, perennial spurs offers the possibility of building up a permanent geometrical scaffold covered with long-lived fruiting buds, eventually leading to the various Espalier forms.

This is different with Stone fruits like Peaches, Plums and Cherries but that's a story for another day.

Leaders do best in the vertical and fruiting laterals do best in the horizontal or even cascading downwards, as in the Spindle method. As an Espalier matures, thinning the abundant fruit becomes one of the most important jobs in June and July.

Now can you see all the Espalier possibilities in this starter nursery tree?   The Single Cordon, U, Double-U, The Fan and others are lying in wait for the Espalier artist to bring them into form.

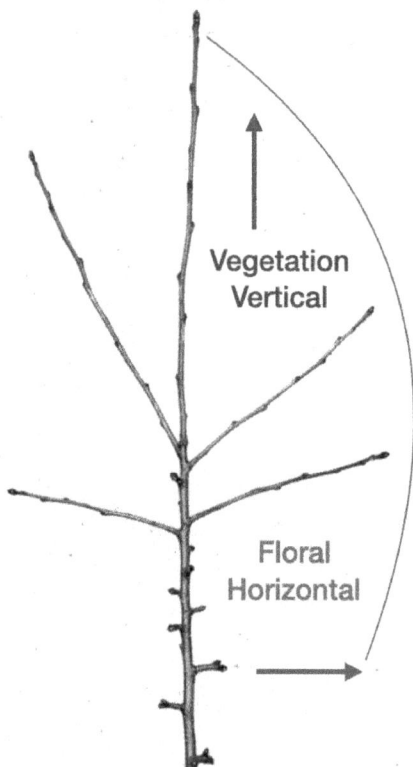

Vegetation
Vertical

Floral
Horizontal

Empty space between leaders are important for air and light leading to quality and health.

That space also makes inspection, thinning, and other treatments easy and accessible.

Energy flows in through the vegetation and flows out through the flowers and fruits.

Chapter 2 Rootstocks & Grafting

Even though I know how to graft and propagate rootstocks, it's still a wonderful mystery that continues to fascinate me.

For the webinar I just focused on the fact that when you buy an Apple tree you are actually making a *dual purchase*: The *variety* with the pretty picture on the label, also known as the scion and the *rootstock* which is often not identified.

It's important for anyone about to plant an apple tree to recognize and locate the graft union - where the stock and scion were grafted together - as it should be ~3 inches above soil level. Otherwise there's a chance that the scion starts forming its own roots and bypassing any benefit the selected rootstock was intended to provide such as dwarfing, early fruiting or precocity, disease resistance, and so on. I've seen it happen.

In one of the orchards I cared for this happened with quite a few trees and the orchard was delayed in fruiting and overgrew, creating massive shadow problems that made it unreachable, all because they were planted too deep and the scions reverted to 'standard' rootstocks versus the semi-dwarf stocks originally purchased.

Older orchards used standard stocks planted on 20' squares for 100 trees per acre. These trees would easily get 24'-30' tall. It's rare to see such orchards today, but it's fairly common to see single trees in backyards that are equally challenging. Here is the spectrum of tradeoffs in choosing a rootstock from 100% standard size to 35% dwarfing. Most Espalier uses <60% and spindle <40% size.

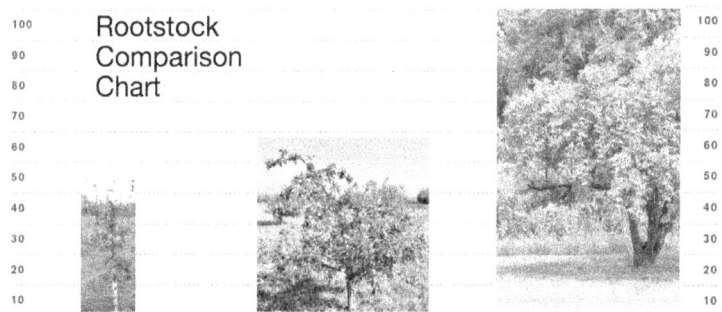

Rootstock Comparison Chart

Dwarfing	Semi-dwarfing	Standard/Seedling

⬅️ ➡️

Need Support	Self Supporting
Earlier Fruiting	Later Fruiting
Less Drought Tolerant	More Drought Tolerant
Easier Access	Harder Access

There are situations where you might want >60% size, such as in drought or other extremely challenging environments for the deeper root system. But this takes us outside of the topic of small trees and you will need ladders to access your tree.

How rootstocks are propagated

You've probably seen suckers arising from the base of a tree. If it's a grafted tree they are likely rootstock suckers and not the same as the scion variety. This happens on other nursery propagated ornamentals with choice varieties. If you carefully dig out and remove these suckers you can grow them on for a year and graft them with scions of your choice and create a new nursery plant yourself.

The Cornell research station at Geneva NY has been a pioneer in breeding, testing, and releasing new rootstock varieties for the benefit of mostly commercial growers. Once they are ready for public release, licensed growers can propagate these paying a royalty to Cornell, the patent holder. After 20 years when the patent comes off, they come into the public domain and can be propagated by the public freely. This is true for new Varieties as well as rootstocks.

Rootstocks are propagated in what's called 'stool mounds or rows' where the mother plant is cut down to create a bunch of suckers, which are then mounded up with soil so the suckers already begin forming roots in the first season. In the Fall, these partially rooted suckers are cut away, and planted out. The soil is removed from the mother mound and the process is repeated year after year.

These rootstocks are later grafted and a new grafted stock/scion combo is created. Both stocks and scions are thus vegetatively propagated, keeping the genetic characteristics intact for predictable performance of both the rootstock below and the variety above.

Yet both began as seedlings. Out of thousands of seedlings a handful advance to further testing and trials before public release. As with all seedlings there is the potential for something entirely new and never seen before. This is the beauty of the biology of the flowering kingdom: to create opportunities for evolutionary diversity.

Dwarfing rootstocks are essential to modern orcharding systems, including the spindle form, that look more like vineyards than the orchards of the past.

I used to think dwarfing rootstocks were smaller because they were weaker...

I've since come to appreciate the many characteristics that the rootstock choice confers to the entire tree, including early fruiting, wider angled branching, and certain resistances to various diseases. It's not that the dwarfing influence is weaker, but is in part a result of early fruiting that transforms shoots and woody growth into fruit, making for a smaller tree. This goes along with the understanding that Pome fruit is modified wood allowing resources to be directed into either fruits or shoots. At maturity the entire tree has an umbrella form of cascading laterals covered in fruit. Whether it is 9' tall or 29' tall, it reflects that spectrum rootstock choice.

This is why thinning fruit is so important in helping regulate the balance between depleting the trees' resources by over-fruiting and encouraging the right amoußnt of early fruiting to slow down size and establish a good presence of flower buds.

Thinning Fruits

Cherries ~5 leaves per fruit.
Plums ~ 10 leaves per fruit.
Apples ~25 leaves per fruit.
Peaches ~35 leaves per fruit.

Thinning fruit helps achieve a *healthy balance* between the rejuvenating influence of vegetation and the depleting influence of fruiting.

Rule of thumb- a single sized fruit gap between fruits.

Modern research confirms ideal leaf/fruit ratios for different types of fruit to help determine thinning formulas (See chart) and annual **cropping targets:**

- Year 1 < 5 fruits
- Year 2 < 20 fruits
- Year 3 < 40 fruits
- Year 4 < 70 fruits
- Year 5 < 90 fruits

The Art of Espalier arose before many of the dwarfing rootstocks we take for granted were available. Espalier artists instead used various techniques, including: dividing the leader into multiple stems, bending laterals, and heavier than typical cropping targets to reduce the overall vigor in the absence of dwarfing rootstock options.

Monsieur Lorette used this with pear trees in France in the late 19th and early 20th centuries with impressive results. Pears, although Pome fruits like apples, are different, and for this booklet and webinar I've chosen to focus on apples.

With both Espalier and the spindle method, due to the use of dwarfing rootstocks, a strong trellis system needs to be installed at the time of planting since the heavy cropping will cause the trees to lean or even fall over. Although this increases the initial cost of installation, its value is soon realized in quantity, quality, and accessibility of fruit. As a Garden teacher I found this last point especially valuable for school and community gardens where people of all ages and abilities could literally get closer to the trees.

Trellis Design

If you have more than five trees you'll need a strong trellis. The industry standard is very similar to high tensile fencing used for livestock, only without electrification. If you're putting in a trellis you might want to research local agricultural fencing companies for tools, supplies, and equipment. In Pennsylvania, when I was putting in 800' of trellis I found *Kencove Fencing* and *Tractor Supply* good resources.

I was surprised to learn that in order to have a trellis 8' tall you would need a post 12' tall so that one-third of the post would be in the ground. And if you are stringing four high tension wires you will need to create an 'end brace' section so that the end post doesn't pull out of the ground or bend under the high tension much like the tension of musical instrument strings.

This might all sound like overkill but the point is the trellis needs to fit your situation, which may also have aesthetic components including walls, fences, and buildings, etc.

Below is a homemade end brace with a diagonal tension wire and a horizontal post pinned in with 1/2" rebar pins pre-drilled. See 5 Easy Steps at https://kencove.com/fence/113_single+end+brace_resource.php

Chapter 3 Varieties

Apple growers have thousands of varieties to choose from. At one school in California I planted sixty heirloom varieties.

Yet when I moved to Pennsylvania I discovered more pests and diseases than I ever knew existed. I began to appreciate the efforts that have gone into breeding varieties with natural resistance to various diseases.

Start a research wish list and make note of the following factors to narrow down your choice. Here's a criteria list I put together for Zone 5, Northern Colorado.

Narrow down variety choices by:

- Disease resistance: CAR, Fireblight, PM, Scab
- Hardiness: Your Zone or hardier
- Pollination Season: Later group, #3 or 4 to escape frost
- Pollinator: At least 3 compatible pollinators
- Heat tolerance
- Earlier ripening: October or before
- Uses: Fresh, Storability, Cider, Drying, Culinary.
- Others: Heirloom, Specialty, Size.

Cummins Nursery is a great resource for information on a wide variety of choices. There is no one perfect variety and experimentation is great. But why grow a variety that is just going to frustrate you with its susceptibility to Cedar Apple rust, etc... and cost you a lot of time and money.

If you want, make a spreadsheet with these notes as well as links for sources and more. Here's a sample spreadsheet-

Variety	Bl. #	Ripen (NY)	Uses	Disease	Notes
Akane	4	Sept. 1	Fresh Culinary	Apple Maggot Susceptible Fireblight Resistant Cedar-Apple Rust Resistant Powdery Mildew Resistant Apple Scab Very Resistant Anthracnose Canker and Bull's-eye Rot Very Susceptible	Cold Hardy- Zone 4 Heat Tolerant
Alkmene	2	Sept.8	Fresh Culinary	Apple Scab Resistant PM Resistant Fireblight Susceptible	Cold Hardy- Zone 5 Heat Tolerant AKA – Early Windsor
Centennial	3	Aug. 18	Fresh Culinary	Apple Scab Resistant Fireblight Resistant	Very Cold Hardy- Zone 3 Heat Tolerant. Crab
Chestnut Crab	3	Sept. 1	Fresh Culinary Cider	Apple Scab Very Resistant Fireblight Resistant	Cold Hardy- Zone 3 Heat Tolerant Weeping. Keeps 1-3 mo.
Crimson Topaz	3	Oct. 13	Fresh Culinary	Powdery Mildew Resistant Apple Scab Resistant	Cold Hardy- Zone 5 Heat Tolerant Keeps 1-3 months
Galarina	3	Oct. 9	Fresh Storage	Fireblight Very Resistant PM Very Resistant Apple Scab Very Resistant	Hot climate tolerant Hardy- Zone 4 Disease resistant

In the first column is variety name. Then: Bloom Group 1-Early to 4-Late; Ripening Date based on NY (Since I was using Cummins site); Uses; Some Disease info.; and other Notes. Create something that works for you to focus your choices on those with the greatest potential for success and satisfaction.

As the Backyard Fruit Growers https://byfg.org/ bumper sticker says:

Too many Apples - Too little time

You can also explore local orchards and groups to find regional expertise and experience that will be helpful in choosing varieties. *Warning* - there are even more opinions out there than there are varieties.

Planning for Success and Health

By puttering around your small trees and Espalier, odds are problems will come to your attention sooner, both because you're paying closer attention *and* your trees are so much more accessible.

On your Espalier trees with 18"-24" between leaders, thinning fruit to the right cropping targets, along with good air circulation already reduces the spread of disease spores while leaving room for various physical, biological, organic, and chemical (if you prefer) treatments as needed.

In addition to the better light and air circulation that the open spacing allows, you can see pests and diseases earlier so you can begin identification/diagnosis and treatments. A good gardener is a vigilant student of Nature. Because Espalier is so beautiful and interesting to look at - you are more likely to be a constant student with a small tree than a large one.

As with all gardening, soil, water, and ecological partnerships also play a role in supporting success and health.

Pests/Disease Tend to Trouble Stressed Plants

An ounce of prevention is worth a pound of cure, to quote Benjamin Franklin. Although these are each worthy of a webinar on their own below is a brief description.

Soil health	Mulch, Compost, Teas, etc
Water movement	Drainage and irrigation
Air circulation	Spacing between branches
Light	Min. 8 hours/day at equinox
Climate Zone	Hardiness, pollination category
Aspect/Exposure	North/East/South/West

At one garden I visited recently, in a forest setting which is lovely, there was not enough light. Many of our cultivated garden plants may grow in lower light. yet don't flower and fruit as well as they could.

In some regions it was common to plant orchards on a Northern slope to delay blooming too early and losing fruit to early spring frosts. Gentle slopes also can avoid frost pockets. Alan York used to say "Fruit trees like a good view." Again, learn from old-timers and local folks when you can.

Along with proper pruning and training, all these cultural practices will contribute to the health and success of your small apple trees.

If you find a certain variety is too problematic or never fruits, you can always graft a more adapted variety to it. This is called top-working when you graft high up in the tree and can lead to multiple varieties on a single tree. It can be tricky to keep track of labels, so take a lot of pictures and soon you will begin to recognize different varieties even without labels especially when in fruit.

Chapter 4 The Tall Spindle Method

Why is the tall spindle method *the* standard for modern orcharding?

Because it is the most productive system for quick returns on your investment.

It is similar to Espalier in that it uses dwarfing rootstocks, trellises, and is very efficient and accessible. Yet the spindle is different - in that the fruiting laterals are much longer than Espalier giving a bushy or weeping gesture versus the sharp geometry of Espalier.

The other big difference is the tall spindle is most often used in high-density mono-cultural plantings with over 1,000 trees per acre. Still, if you had 9 of these trees you might even be more satisfied than if you had 3 or 4 Espalier.

Why? Because they have the potential of fruiting sooner and thus keeping your interest engaged so you don't give up. This gets you hooked on the joy of small trees sooner.

There's no reason why you can't have some of both. And when you know both systems, you'll apply techniques from both systems to your advantage and situation.

As hinted at earlier, dwarfing rootstocks really work well with the longer weeping laterals of the spindle tree. Modern dwarfing rootstocks have been selected especially for spindle orchards. Because of this, the spindle actually requires less work than Espalier with its focus on many short spur-laterals versus spindle trees.

I confess, had I known about it earlier I would have included it in all my educational, community, and backyard gardens long ago, simply because the learning curve and tenacity is so much more demanding with Espalier.

Even though many of the principles from Espalier apply to the spindle it's actually a very different mindset to go from the more crystalline form of the Espalier to a kind of bush-on-a-stick form where you renew a few 5-year old laterals annually for maintenance after 6 years onwards.

That means, unlike all the summer branch manipulation of Espalier, the tall spindle can get away with two *Bevel Cuts* in winter and you're done. Which is how growers with thousands of trees manage to do it.

Currently there is a speciality wholesale supply chain used mainly by wholesale growers who buy quality trees grown especially for high-density plantings in lots of 500 or 1,000. While retail nurseries often sell trees not suited for the Spindle method.

Once the Spindle method is widely understood I think it will awaken a whole new generation to the joy of growing small Apple trees.

I also imagine that master gardeners and nurseries will start advocating and teaching the Spindle method, since it is too good to ignore.

I'm going to break my own rule - *of not repeating what was already said in the webinar* - and repeating it here for your study and consideration, since it is such a different mindset to either Espalier or older standard orcharding systems. I think folks with orchards will start to look at their trees with fresh eyes.

The Spindle

Has a similar form to a tree 10x its age in 1/10th the space!!!

A five year old spindle relaxes into near total fruit similar to a tree ten times its age. It has a minimal leader scaffold and upright growth and maximal cascading laterals.

With older trees, many folks take the approach of *Renovation Pruning* which involves a lot of major cuts to let in light and stimulate new growth, starting over.

Yet one could take a similar approach as spindle maintenance pruning does with older trees: thinning ~10% of the now large cascading Laterals each year, starting in the middle, and working up. Basically: judicious thinning.

But I'm getting ahead of myself, yet wanted to offer the view that the umbrella form of the older tree is not always a sign of decline. Let's compare a slender tall spindle with a single cordon pear espalier.

Espalier vs. Tall Spindle

Formal	Informal
Slower to fruit 5+ yrs	Faster to fruit 2+ yrs
More complex	Less complex
Retains 'tree' Character	More 'shrub-like'
Perennial laterals- pinching and bending	Renewable laterals- using the *'Bevel cut'*.

In the webinar I described the spindle as: less formal, faster to fruit, less complex, more shrub-like, with longer laterals that are renewed using a pruning cut unique to the Spindle method- The *Bevel Cut*.

The Bevel Cut

Goes against any good rose pruners' training, yet in this case - the intention is initiating a new cascading lateral that in consort with the dwarfing rootstock may set flower buds at the end of year one and bear fruit in year two. I compare this system of renewing laterals, as similar to renewing bramble canes after two year and climbing rose canes after four years. The difference being the spindle is a woody tree - not a shrub - so renewal occurs along the trunk and not at the base like a shrub.

Building up the Spindle Tree

The first 5 years is very similar to the Single Cordon Espalier.

Year 1

Start with a healthy, preferably large grade or caliper nursery tree on a dwarfing rootstock (Not semi-dwarf – See Chapter 2)

Remove any co-dominant branches that are 55% or greater than the main trunk using the bevel cut.

Leave the leader uncut or cut maximum ~10% if flimsy and tie to a vertical support.

Install a single stake for the single trunk. Note: you can use a length of bamboo if you're also installing a trellis. If a single, or trio to be united for rigidity, it's preferable to use a top of the line stake such as https://www.amleo.com/fiberglass-tree-stakes-8-year-life-8-feet-x-5-8-inches-bundle-of-10/p/ES5808-10 Remember 18-24" will go in the ground.

Bend all other laterals down, preferably below horizontal as shown in Module 1 of the webinar using wires, rubber bands, clothes pins, whatever does the trick. New techniques are popping up all the time for this. The goal here is to set flower buds by July/August to fruit next year. At which time the (thinned) fruit will do the bending for you.

Years 2-5

Continue to train single leader to the top or just a little beyond and bend down or allow fruit to bend it down.

Remove any big branches greater than 66% of the main trunk using the Bevel Cut.

Shorten older laterals to a weak point or fruit spur.

Follow cropping targets and thinning protocol.

Years 6 and beyond. Maintaining the Spindle

By now the central trunk is the main woody spindle from which around 20 long weeping laterals are loaded with fruit.

A main task with the laterals is thinning the fruit in July after any natural 'June drop' is finished to allow the remaining crop to fully ripen and color up.

Bevel cut renewal begins by removing 10% of the oldest, largest laterals. These are likely to be in the middle as legacy branches from the early days. You might only remove two using the Bevel replace cut. This will allow light and air to reach the remaining laters.

The goal here is to keep renewing small laterals. You want to avoid large branches or vigorous shoots that will stimulate too much vegetative growth.

You're going for that weeping umbrella look of a tree much older than it actually is.

It will still need support, either a trellis or strong stake. Or the trio idea.

In the webinar I showed how I started to change over an older orchard to the Spindle method. I would never go back to the big trees. I simply love how you can get close to your trees without a ladder.

How might one incorporate the Spindle form into a garden rather than an orchard?

Use the trio technique with spacing three trees ~3-4 feet apart and put in support stakes for each, uniting them with cross supports making a vertical triangular pillar - now no need for a big trellis structure - but individual trios.

And using three varieties will help with pollination and add a range of harvesting dates - a win/win. Three such trios will give you a mini-orchard with nine varieties in a small space that is easy to access.

As much as I love Espalier, I've come to appreciate the advantages of the spindle: sooner to fruit, less formal and thus looking more natural, and more forgiving in terms of maintenance pruning.

Both the spindle and espalier need support structures due to the heavy fruiting.

Once you are familiar with both systems to can apply aspects of each to the other and achieve wonderful results from your small apple trees.

Chapter 5 Making it Your Own

No matter whether you take on Espalier or the spindle method - You will make it your own. And therein lies the joy and adventure of growing small apple trees and even reaping rewards that you may not have sought out for in the first place, such as discovering heirloom culinary varieties, donating varieties with good storing qualities to local food banks, supporting pollinator bees, and sharing your knowledge with others.

You might start planting small apple trees because you want local healthy foods, or bring horticulture to local schools, community gardens, senior centers, or therapeutic programs. No matter where you start, I promise you will discover the joys of all these harvests and much more.

We start out cultivating the garden and discover it is cultivating us and it's all for the better in ways we never imagined. No wonder Gardening enchants more and more gardeners every year. Let this be a new year for you.

One of my greatest joys has been teaching gardening and high school science at the Kimberton Waldorf School in Pennsylvania - a K-12 program growing young people through the craft, art, and science of horticulture.

As trees grow, so do you. Plant curiosity, cultivate responsibility, and harvest care

As I've gone on to give classes to adults, I've found gardening doesn't stop in Kindergarten... the same principles apply to all gardeners whether at home, in a school, or community garden.

Gardening awakens Interest in the World. And Interest in turn - awakens Responsibility. Such Responsibility matures into Love.

This is how gardening is a metaphor for growing anything - a child, a family, community and culture. This will happen for you as you gain success with growing your small apple trees. The greatest harvest you will reap is when you share this with friends, family and community.

This is the superpower of apples trees - More than most other tree fruits - they are adapted to storing and therefore traveling well within your community. Again this is due to the unique qualities of Pome fruit as modified wood.

Lastly, if you have questions about your particular trees or location do reach out as I offer a limited number of virtual consults and tutorials. Connect at manzanitatlc.com

Manzanitatlc.com

The Power of
Small Trees

About the Author

Mason Vollmer is a speaker, author and consultant on gardens that grows people.

He has helped establish a variety of horticultural programs including at the: Summefield and Kimberton K–12 Waldorf Schools in California and Pennsylvania; Camphill Soltane in PA: a Living, Learning, and Working Community inclusive to adults with developmental differences; and several other community programs.

He is an advocate of gardening that nourishes the body, soul, and spirit while also helping the environment, society and the planet.

www.ingramcontent.com/pod-product-compliance
Lightning Source LLC
Chambersburg PA
CBHW070206060426
42445CB00033B/1760